Prolance

www.prolancewriting.com
California, USA

Edited by Hadeer Sahar Soliman

©2013 Islam4families.com
ISBN-13: 978-0-9885070-3-6
Printed in USA

Table of Contents:

Preface:

In 1998, when Christmas, Hanukkah, and Ramadan were all celebrated during the month of December, I took my three children, 9-year-old Hadeer, 8-year-old Siraj and 6-year-old Janna to Story Time at the local library.

With great excitement, the librarian told the wide-eyed children that she would read to them stories about the holidays taking place in December: Christmas and Hanukkah.

My daughter, Hadeer, almost automatically, said to me, "How about Ramadan, Mommy? That's in December, too."

After Story Time was over, I asked the librarian to share with the children a story about Ramadan, because the holidays coincided this year.

The librarian retorted, "Ramadan is not a fun month; it's religious."

I proceeded to tell her that, like Christmas and Hanukkah, Ramadan is also a religious time, and that it is, in fact, fun, just like those two holidays.

After a long discussion on this matter, the librarian agreed. If I could bring her a children's story about Ramadan, she would share it during Story Time at the library.

Naturally, I looked in the library for a children's short story about Ramadan.

However, to my children's disappointment and mine, there were none.

That is when I began working with my children on building on their own experiences to write a story about Ramadan.

I also designed an art project for the children to participate in during Story Time the following week at the library.

Elhamdulilah, we were ready that week with a story to share with the children, and we made a lantern as the library's art project for the week.

The following year, when I started teaching and developing the Islamic Studies curriculum at New Horizon School in Los Angeles, Calif., I asked my students to write short stories about Ramadan.

I also requested that they write poems about the Quran, Ramadan, Eid, the Prophet Mohammad (pbuh), and thankfulness.

I then worked on developing creative art projects to bring to life Islamic ideals and help us celebrate Islamic holidays.

Not only did we relate existing arts and crafts projects to Islam, but we also created new ideas and taught the students to relate everything we used to the One who created the materials: God. We taught them that all man-made items are ultimately from God's natural creations.

As an example, we asked the students what wax is made of and encouraged them to do their research and come back to class with an answer. "

Wax is made from natural things like cattle fat, sugars, and honey," they wrote. Then we asked them what people use wax for. "People use wax for things like crayons, candles, and cosmetics," they'd answer. We wanted to clarify to the students that by using their creativity and God's creations, they could produce beautiful art!

Then, from 2011 to 2013, I worked with a designer and editor to publish these four projects into children's books.

**All four books are available at
www.islam4families.com**

I hope my story will encourage other parents to work with their local communities and inspire their children to be proud of and to use their resources to develop their Muslim American identities.

~ Sahar Abdel-Aziz

Introduction:

The signs of Allah's existence are apparent in every aspect of our lives. Because they are so numerous, they are sometimes easy to take for granted.

According to the Quran, every Muslim should seek out these signs.

We should look around us and reflect upon the creation and its purpose. Increasing our awareness in such a manner strengthens our faith and brings us closer to the Creator, Allah.

Here are a few important passages from the Quran about the signs of Allah:

Behold! In the creation of the heavens and the earth; in the alternation of the night and the day; in the sailing of the ships through the ocean for the profit of mankind; in the rain that Allah sends down from the skies, and the life which He gives therewith to an earth that is dead; in the beasts of all kinds that He scatters through the earth; in the change of the winds, and the clouds which they trail like their slaves between the sky and the earth; here indeed are signs for a people that are wise [Al-Baqara:164].

Do you not see that Allah sends down rain from the sky and makes it flow as springs (and rivers) in the earth; then He produces thereby crops of varying colors; then they dry and you see them turned yellow; then He makes them (scattered) debris. Indeed in that is a reminder for those of understanding [Az-Zumar:21].

It is Allah who created the heavens and the earth and sent down rain from the sky and produced thereby some fruits as provision for you and subjected for you the ships to sail through the sea by His command and subjected for you the rivers [Ibrahim:32].

In examining these signs of Allah, we can better understand the different schemes of life. We understand the answers to complex questions, such as:

● Who could be great enough to create the magnificent stars in the sky and also the tiny grains of pollen on a flower?

● Who could be mighty enough to create the earth with its mountains, rivers, and seas?

● What causes heavy ships to float on water? If you place a tiny iron nail in the water, it will sink. But if put a large iron ship in the water, it will stay afloat. Why?

5

● Clouds are made of water. Water is heavier than air. How does so much water get up into the sky? And why doesn't it fall all at once?

● What causes water to bring seeds to life? Why does the earth have so much water? Two-thirds of the earth is covered by water (the sea). What is the wisdom in that?

● Why are there so many different kinds of animals and plants? What gives them their individual characteristics?

● What causes the winds to change? Why don't they always blow in the same direction around the world?

● Who could create the human brain with all its complexities?

Some may say that all of these things happen as a result of nature. The question arises: What is nature? The word "nature" is used to describe certain basic behavior.

For example, the nature of an ant is to live in colonies. The nature of a bee is to make honey. The nature of a bird is to fly and sing.

By the Islamic definition, "nature" characterizes the Signs of Allah. We praise Him for all His signs that we see in the world around us by saying:

ﺑِﺴْـﻢِ ﺍﻟﻠَّﻪِ ﺍﻟﺮَّﺣْﻤَﻦِ ﺍﻟﺮَّﺣِﻴﻢِ ﴿١﴾

ﺍﻟْﺤَﻤْﺪُ ﻟِﻠَّﻪِ ﺭَﺏِّ ﺍﻟْﻌَﺎﻟَﻤِﻴﻦَ ﴿٢﴾

In the name of Allah, the Entirely Merciful, the Especially Merciful. All praise is due to Allah, Lord of the worlds [Al-Fatihah:1-2].

Allah exists. Without comparing Allah to the creation one can use common sense to prove the existence of the Creator. When one sees a building, one knows there is a builder, when one sees a painting, one knows there is a painter, when one sees a creation, one knows there is a creator.

Consider this story: "God, are you real?" A girl whispered, "God, speak to me." And a humming bird sang. But she did not hear. So she yelled," God, speak to me!" And thunder rolled across the sky. But she did not listen. She looked around and said, "God, let me see you." And a star shone brightly. But the girl did not notice. And she shouted, "God show me a miracle!" And a baby was born. But the girl did not know. So she cried out in despair, "Touch me God, and let me know you are here!" At which point God reached down and touched her. But the girl brushed the butterfly away, and walked away unknowingly.

Often times, the things we seek are right underneath our noses. Don't miss out on your blessings because they aren't packaged the way that you expect.

Activity:

Think about your life and create a collage of your blessings. Cut out pictures of your blessings from magazines and glue them on a piece of construction paper.

If you cannot find pictures for your blessings, you can cut out letters from the magazines to form words. Have fun and be creative!

On a separate piece of paper write this verse and paste it into your collage: O you who believe! Celebrate the praises of Allah, and do so often. And glorify Him morning and evening. He it is who sends blessings on you... [Al-'Ahzab:41-42].

7

Chapter 1:
Allah Created Everything

Lesson: Allah brings things into existence; He is the creator of all things, including heaven and earth.

How did the world come into existence? Where did the heavens and earth come from? Have you ever looked at the sky at night? What have you noticed?

You may have seen the moon, round like a ball at times and thin like the tip of a fingernail at others. By observing its changes, we can count the days of the month. You may also have seen thousands of stars in the sky. If you tried to count them all, you would never finish.

Everyday, we see the sun rise in the East and set in the West. With its light, we wake up, we can see the world, and do our work. The same light and warmth causes the plants to grow and the fruits to ripen.

Have you ever wondered where the sun, the moon, the stars, and the earth come from? This is an important question. Did anybody make them, or did they make themselves? Does the sun have a brain?

Could it have made itself? Could it generate its own energy? Does the moon have a brain? Could it know how to change its shape as the days of the month go by? Does the earth have a brain? Does it know how to make the air,

the water, the plants, and the animals?

We know that the sun, the moon, the earth, and the stars do not have a brain. They could not make themselves. If they did not make themselves, then who made them? The name of that Maker of the heavens and the earth is Allah. The Quran says:

$$ تَبَارَكَ ٱلَّذِى جَعَلَ فِى ٱلسَّمَآءِ بُرُوجًا وَجَعَلَ فِيهَا سِرَٰجًا وَقَمَرًا مُّنِيرًا ۝ ٦١ $$

Blessed is He who has placed in the sky great stars and placed therein a [burning] lamp and luminous moon [Al-Furqan:61].

What caused the world and all the living things to come into existence? Who made the first chicken, apple, or man? Who causes them to stay alive and to reproduce themselves right up until this day?

It is Allah, the Creator of the heavens and the earth. In the Quran, He is called Al-Hayy, The Living One. He is the Giver of life. He is also called Al-Rabb, The Sustainer, which means the One Who keeps things alive and provides for all their needs.

And so, every day, we thank Allah with the words of Surah Al-Fatihah:

$$ ٱلْحَمْدُ لِلَّهِ رَبِّ ٱلْعَٰلَمِينَ ۝ ٢ $$

Allah is the One God, the Creator of all that is in the heavens and the earth. Yet, Allah was not created by anyone or anything. He has always existed and will always exist. Allah is called Al-Awwal and Al-Akhir, which means "The First and The Last."

Human beings are very intelligent, but they cannot create something out of nothing. A carpenter may say, "I have made a chair." Yet, they cannot make a chair without wood or metal. They can only use what Allah has created. A baker may say, "I have made a cake." But, they cannot make a cake without flour, eggs, butter, and sugar. They cannot create a cake out of nothing.

Only Allah has the power to create something out of nothing. Allah has another name in the Quran, Al-Khaliq, that means The Creator.

This trait is powerfully established in the following verse of the Quran:

$$\text{إِنَّمَآ أَمۡرُهُۥٓ إِذَآ أَرَادَ شَیۡـًٔا أَن}$$

$$\text{یَقُولَ لَهُۥ كُن فَیَكُونُ ۝}$$

His command is only when He intends a thing that He says to it, "Be," and it is [Ya-Sin:82].

Chapter 1:

Activities

Poems

&

Exercises

Activity:

Decode using 3-shift cipher (A=D, B=E, C=F, etc)

How did God create everything?
DLA PXVP, "YB," XKA FQ FP.

A	B	C	D	E	F	G
D	E	F	G	H	I	J

H	I	J	K	L	M	N
K	L	M	N	O	P	Q

O	P	Q	R	S	T	U
R	S	T	U	V	W	X

V	W	X	Y	Z
Y	Z	A	B	C

Write your answer here:

_____

_____

_____

Exercises:

1 Who is the Creator of the heavens and earth? Who made living things, and who keeps things alive?

2 Write two Arabic words describing Allah with their English translations.

3 Test whether you can create something out of nothing. Wish for a cake or a bike and say, "Be!" Are you able to create something out of nothing? Try to think of something that a human being can create out of nothing? Is there anything?

4 Look at a doll or toy animal. It has the shape of an animal, but is it alive? Can it see? Can it hear? Can it eat? Can it breathe? Can it run? Can anyone give life to that toy? Can you make a toy that is alive? Can a man create a living flower, animal, or human being?

5 Write two names of God that indicate that He is the Creator.

6 Write the names of God that mean He is The First and The Last.

7 Write the verse that says if God wills it, it happens. What is the name of the Surah and the number of the Ayah?

Poem:
Beautiful Works of Allah

All things bright and beautiful
All creatures great and small
All things wise and wonderful
God has made them all.

Each little flower that opens
Each little bird that sings
He made their glowing colors
He made their tiny wings.

The purple-headed mountains
The rivers running by
The sunset and the morning
That brightens up the sky.

All bring a certain message
Of His love to every creature
Each creature is an open page
Of His book the wonderful nature.

Internet Activity:

Watch a video about nature. Then go outside and collect as many different kinds of flowers and leaves that you can find.

We learned that only Allah could create something from nothing and give life. Now let's take a closer look at some of the things that Allah has created. Look at the different flowers and leaves that you collected. Are they all the same? You will notice many differences.

- Compare the SIZE of the flowers and leaves.
- Compare their SHAPES. Some are round, some long, some shaped like fans, knives, stars, bells, or trumpets.
- Compare their COLORS. How many different colors do you see?
- Compare their SMELL. Some are sweet and some are not. Some have no scent.
- Compare their TEXTURE. Some are hard, soft, thick, fleshy, thin, etc.

Then answer these questions by writing a paragraph: 1. Why aren't they all the same? 2. Who has made them different from one another? Think about the animals you know. If you begin naming them, you will never finish because there are so many. 3. Why are there so many different kinds of animals?

Allah has answered this question in the Quran. He says He creates what He likes, and that He is never tired of creating. He is called Al-Bari and Al-Musawwir, The Maker and The Fashioner. Which means the One who gives things their shape and their way of being. Allah is all-powerful. Think of all the things in the heavens and the earth that were created and given its own unique shape by Him. Who or what can we compare with Allah? Indeed there is nothing that can be compared with Him. Allah says that even the sun, the moon, the stars, and the earth had a beginning and will one day have an end.

Only Allah has no beginning and no end. He is limitless. Allah is not a created thing, and He is not like the things He created. Allah also has the name Al-Baqi, which means The Everlasting. Everything on earth will die, but Allah exists forever. He says in the Quran: Everyone upon the earth will perish. And there will remain the Face of your Lord, Owner of Majesty and Honor [Al-Rahman:26-27].

كُلُّ مَنْ عَلَيْهَا فَانٍ ﴿٢٦﴾

وَيَبْقَىٰ وَجْهُ رَبِّكَ ذُو الْجَلَالِ وَالْإِكْرَامِ ﴿٢٧﴾

Exercises:

1 Who created things with different forms?

2 Write the name of God in Arabic that means God is never tired.

3 Why is it useless to worship someone other than Allah?

4 Write the name of God in Arabic that means God makes things in different forms?

5 Do all the plants and animals you know die?

6 Is there any creature that lives forever?

Poem: Allah, Allah

Who gives life, who takes life?
Allah, Allah

Who takes life. And gives again?
Allah, Allah

Who gives mother, who gives father?
Allah, Allah

Who gives sweets, who gives toys?

Allah, Allah

Lord of all, friend of all.
Allah, Allah

Pray to Him, to Him alone.
Allah, Allah

Make us wise, make us good.
Allah, Allah

18

Activity:

God created many things for mankind to use to make our lives better. Some of these things He created we call "natural resources" like water, soil, sand, coal. For thousands of years, man has used these resources to improve life in his community. If you were a farmer or an automobile maker, certain resources would be more important to you than others.

On this t-graph, list 10 items that God created and 10 things people make with them.

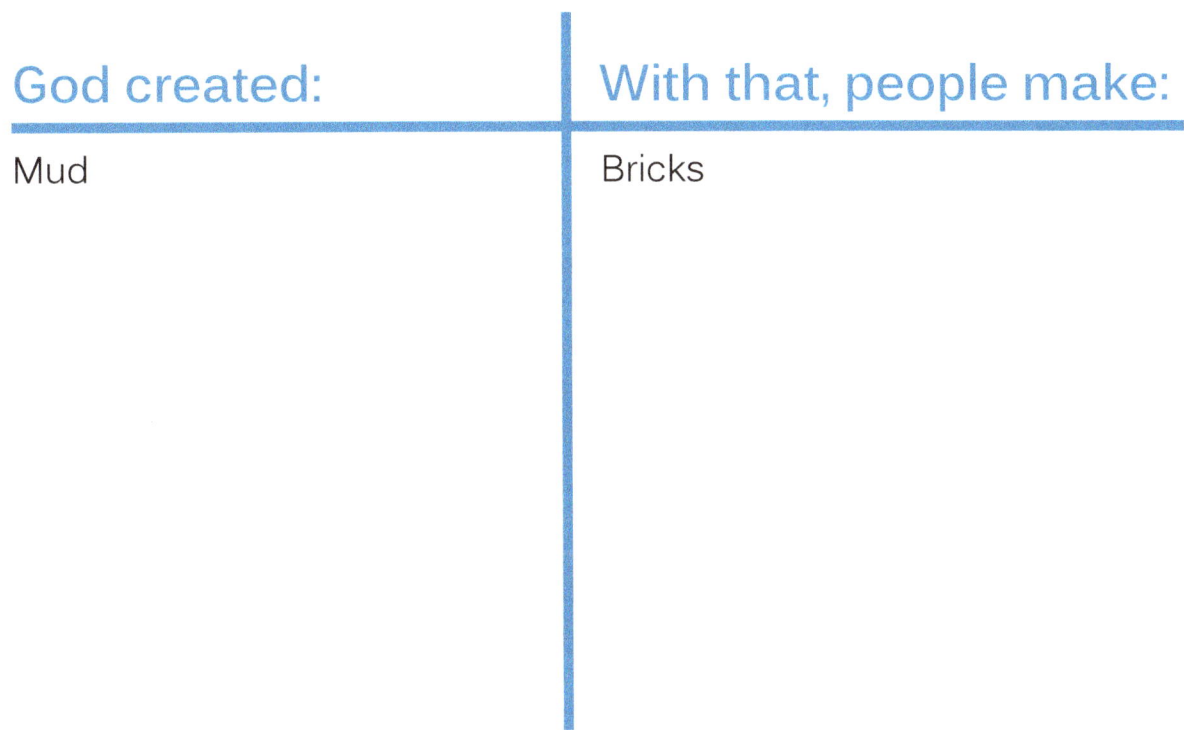

God created:	With that, people make:
Mud	Bricks

Then choose a profession and explain how natural resources are essential for your job. Some examples are: chef, oil driller, coal miner, window manufacturer, fence maker, newspaper publisher, etc. Also, tell how your job helps your community.

Reading:

Allah is the creator. He made us. Allah also created the trees, the oceans, the mountains, and the clouds. Allah even made the little things like insects, bugs, and other tiny animals. Allah also created the big elephants, tigers, whales, and lions. Thus Allah can create anything big or small. Things in the deep oceans and the things on the top of high mountains.

There are some things we see and some things we can't. There are many things in the world that we can see like balloons, light bulbs, and batteries. Then there are other things that we cannot see, like the air in the balloon, the current in the light bulb, and the power in the batteries. We know the air, the current, and the power exists, otherwise the bal-loon would not inflate, the bulb will not light, and the batteries will not work.

We know that Allah created all these things on earth. Allah is all-powerful. He is the maker of everything, the sun, the moon, the sky, the seas, the hills, the trees, the planets, humans, plants, animals, angels, and jinn. When He wants to make anything He says, "Be" and it is made. In the beginning there was only God. There was no sun, sky, moon, or anything. Then He wanted them and they came to life.

Creation of Angels: He made angels to serve Him. They are made out of light. They do not die. They can go anywhere Allah wants them to go. They can do anything Allah wants them to do. Allah has distributed work among them. Some angels are superior to others. They are known as archangels. Jibreel is one of them. He is the angel of life. He is also a messenger. He brings Allah's message to messengers on earth who are human beings. Azrail is another archangel. He is the angel of death. He takes away souls when Allah wants us to leave the earth. There are millions and millions of angels each doing their job.

Creation of the sky: He wanted the sun, moon, stars, and planets to be

made. Then He placed them in the sky and ordered them to move. But He made laws for them. They all follow rules. That is why they do not hit each other.

Creation of animals: He placed animals on this earth. We do not know how many kinds of animals or birds there are. Long ago there were large animals. Some of them, which we call dinosaurs, were very large. We found their skeletons. They died many, many years ago. Allah made monkeys, apes, and gorillas.

Creation of Jinn: They are made of fire. They could take any shape they like. They could become invisible. After their creation, they gradually started misbehaving. They would not pray or have faith. Then Allah punished them. The good jinns believe in Allah, pray to Him and do good deeds. We cannot see them with our eyes unless they take some shape or form.

The Quran says: Allah is the one who created you, then provided for you, then will cause you to die, and then will give you life. Are there any of your "partners" who does anything of that? Exalted is He and high above what they associate with Him [Ar-Rum:40].

And it is He who created the night and the day and the sun and the moon; all (heavenly bodies) in an orbit are swimming [Al-'Anbya':33].

And Allah has made for you, from that which He has created, shadows and has made for you from the mountains, shelters and has made for you garments which protect you from the heat and garments which protect you from your (enemy in) battle. Thus does He complete His favor upon you that you might submit to Him [An-Nahl:81].

Indeed, your Lord is Allah, who created the heavens and the earth in six days and then established Himself above the Throne, arranging the matter [of His creation]. There is no intercessor except after His permission. That is Allah, your Lord, so worship Him. Then will you not remember? [Al-Fil:3].

Do they not look into the realm of the heavens and the earth and everything that Allah has created and (think) that perhaps their appointed time has come near? So in what statement hereafter will they believe? [Al-A'raf:185].

Activity:
The chicken, the mango, and the man:

Ask yourself the following questions:

Q: **Where does a chicken come from?**
A: It comes from an egg.

Q: **Where does the egg come from?**
A: It comes from a chicken.

Q: **Where does that chicken come from?**
A: It comes from another egg.

Q: **Where do you find a mango fruit?**
A: On a mango tree.

Q: **Where did the mango tree come from?**
A: From the seed inside another mango.

Q: **And where did that mango come from?**
A: From another mango tree.

Q: Where did you come from?
A: My mother gave birth to me.
Q: And where did your mother come from?
A: Her mother gave birth to her.

Ask these questions about any living thing and you will get the same pattern of answers. From this we can see that every living thing grew out of something else, and this has happened for thousands of years. But we know that the world has a beginning. And therefore, everything on earth had a beginning. What caused the world and all the living things to exist? What or who made the first chicken, mango, and man? What or who causes them to stay alive and to produce eggs and seeds and babies till this day? It is Allah, the Creator of the Heavens and the Earth.

23

Chapter 2:
Names of Allah

Allah's Names:

Lesson: To learn that Allah has 99 names and how they are attributed to the power of Allah. You will learn how knowing these names will affect your life and experiences.

Allah has many names (attributes). Through His names, we learn of His Power and His traits. This information is useful in learning how to better serve Him. Allah has 99 names. They are found in different parts of the Quran.

There is one particular Ayah of the Quran in which Allah reveals many of His attributes:

هُوَ ٱللَّهُ ٱلَّذِى لَآ إِلَٰهَ إِلَّا هُوَ عَٰلِمُ ٱلْغَيْبِ وَٱلشَّهَٰدَةِ هُوَ ٱلرَّحْمَٰنُ ٱلرَّحِيمُ ﴿٢٢﴾ هُوَ ٱللَّهُ ٱلَّذِى لَآ إِلَٰهَ إِلَّا هُوَ ٱلْمَلِكُ ٱلْقُدُّوسُ ٱلسَّلَٰمُ ٱلْمُؤْمِنُ ٱلْمُهَيْمِنُ ٱلْعَزِيزُ ٱلْجَبَّارُ ٱلْمُتَكَبِّرُ سُبْحَٰنَ ٱللَّهِ عَمَّا يُشْرِكُونَ ﴿٢٣﴾ هُوَ ٱللَّهُ ٱلْخَٰلِقُ ٱلْبَارِئُ ٱلْمُصَوِّرُ لَهُ ٱلْأَسْمَآءُ ٱلْحُسْنَىٰ يُسَبِّحُ لَهُۥ مَا فِى ٱلسَّمَٰوَٰتِ وَٱلْأَرْضِ وَهُوَ ٱلْعَزِيزُ ٱلْحَكِيمُ ﴿٢٤﴾

He is Allah, other than Whom there is no other Allah, the Knower of the Invisible and the Visible. He is the Beneficent, Merciful. He is Allah, than Whom there is no other Allah, the Sovereign Lord, the Holy One, Peace, the Keeper of Faith, the Guardian, the Majestic, the Compeller, the Superb. Glorified be Allah from all that they ascribe as partner (unto Him). He is Allah, the Creator, the Shaper out of naught, the Fashioner. His are the most beautiful names. All that is in the heavens and the earth glorifies Him, and He is the Mighty, the Wise [Al-Hashr:22-24].

Two very important names are found in the Quran repeatedly, and at the beginning of almost every Surah. They are: Al-Rahman and Al-Rahim, The most Gracious and The most Merciful. From these names, we understand the magnitude of Allah's grace and mercy.

We find evidence of this fact in every blessing He has given us. Think about all the things that Allah has done for you. We should remember Allah's blessings to us and be grateful for His mercy.

In another Ayah Allah says:

بِسْمِ اللَّهِ نُورُ السَّمَوَاتِ وَالْأَرْضِ مَثَلُ نُورِهِ كَمِشْكَوةٍ فِيهَا مِصْبَاحٌ الْمِصْبَاحُ فِي زُجَاجَةٍ الزُّجَاجَةُ كَأَنَّهَا كَوْكَبٌ دُرِّيٌّ يُوقَدُ مِن شَجَرَةٍ مُّبَـٰرَكَةٍ زَيْتُونَةٍ لَّا شَرْقِيَّةٍ وَلَا غَرْبِيَّةٍ يَكَادُ زَيْتُهَا يُضِيءُ وَلَوْ لَمْ تَمْسَسْهُ نَارٌ نُّورٌ عَلَىٰ نُورٍ يَهْدِى اللَّهُ لِنُورِهِ مَن يَشَاءُ وَيَضْرِبُ اللَّهُ الْأَمْثَـٰلَ لِلنَّاسِ وَاللَّهُ بِكُلِّ شَيْءٍ عَلِيمٌ ﴿٣٥﴾

Allah is the Light of the heavens and the earth. The example of His light is like a niche within which is a lamp, the lamp is within glass, the glass as if it were a pearly [white] star lit from [the oil of] a blessed olive tree, neither of the east nor of the west, whose oil would almost glow even if untouched by fire. Light upon light. Allah guides to His light whom He wills. And Allah presents examples for the people, and Allah is Knowing of all things [An-Nur:35].

We know that Allah is so great, because He is never far away. He says:

وَقَالَ رَبُّكُمُ ادْعُونِي أَسْتَجِبْ لَكُمْ إِنَّ الَّذِينَ يَسْتَكْبِرُونَ عَنْ عِبَادَتِي سَيَدْخُلُونَ جَهَنَّمَ دَاخِرِينَ ﴿٦٠﴾

And your Lord says, "Call upon Me; I will respond to you." Indeed, those who disdain My worship will enter Hell [rendered] shameful [Ghafir:60].

Moreover, it has been reported that the Prophet (p) said, "Ihsan is to worship Allah as if you see Him, and if you do not achieve this state of devotion, then Allah sees you."

Obviously, it is important that we are conscious of Allah at all times, and that we behave with the full understanding that He is present with us and a Witness to all that we do.

27

Chapter 2:
Activities
Poems
&
Exercises

Activities:

1 In your own words, rephrase the above Ayah of the Quran Al-Hashr:22-24.

2 Memorize Ayah Al-Hashr:22-24 with the help of a family member.

Crossword Puzzle:

A	L	L	A	H	S	D	E	E	J	A	M
K	L	A	L	J	A	L	E	E	L	M	E
H	A	I	E	S	A	M	A	D	E	B	E
I	B	G	E	U	B	Z	E	E	F	A	H
R	A	H	M	A	N	S	Z	E	E	R	A
I	Z	A	A	A	A	Q	A	D	I	R
V	I	F	G	L	W	A	D	O	O	D	A
A	Z	F	A	A	E	B	A	Q	I	B	Z
S	W	A	R	I	S	E	A	A	A	A	Z
S	M	R	K	I	L	A	M	V	H	H	A
U	K	H	A	L	I	Q	H	I	R	A	Q
M	U	N	I	M	E	E	R	A	K	W	U

ALEEM	GHAFFAR	KHALIQ	RAHEEM
ALLAH	HAFEEZ	MAJEED	RAZZAQ
ALI	HALEEM	MALIK	SALAAM
AKHIR	HAI	MUNIM	SAMAD
AZEEM	HAMEED	MUSAWWIR	WUDOOD
AZIZ	HAQ	QADIR	WAHAB
BAQI	JALEEL	QAVI	WARIS
BARI	KAREEM	RAHMAN	ZAHIR

30

Poem:

Allah is He, besides Whom there is no other God
The One who knows both what you cannot see and what you can see
He, Most Gracious, Most Merciful
Allah is He, besides Whom there is no other God

The King, the Holy
The source of peace and salvation
The giver of Faith
The One Who determines what is true and false

The Almighty
The One who subdues wrong and restores right
The Supreme
Glory to Allah

High is He above the partners
That men may attribute Him
He is Allah, the Creator
The Maker who shapes all forms and appearances

His alone are the most beautiful names
All that is in the heavens and on earth
Declares His Praises and Glory
And He is the Almighty, the Wise.

Activity: The 99 Names of Allah:

Choose one of the names from the chart below and write it in Arabic on a poster board to make a painting to hang in your room.

Arabic	Transliteration	Translation
الرحمن	Ar-Rahmān	The All Beneficent
الرحيم	Ar-Rahīm	The Most Merciful
الملك	Al-Malik	The Ultimate King
القدوس	Al-Quddūs	The Most Holy, The Most Pure
السلام	As-Salām	The Peace and Blessing
المؤمن	Al-Mu'min	The Granter of Security
المهيمن	Al-Muhaymin	The Guardian
العزيز	Al-Azīz	The Almighty
الجبار	Al-Jabbār	The Compeller
المتكبر	Al-Mutakabbir	The Tremendous
الخالق	Al-Khāliq	The Creator
البارئ	Al-Bāri'	The Rightful
المصور	Al-Musawwir	The Fashioner of Forms
الغفار	Al-Ghaffār	The Ever Forgiving
القهار	Al-Qahhār	The All Compelling Subduer
الوهاب	Al-Wahhāb	The Bestower
الرزاق	Ar-Razzāq	The Ever Providing
الفتاح	Al-Fattāh	The Opener

العليم	Al-'Alīm	The All Knowing
القابض	Al-Qābid	The Restrainer
الباسط	Al-Bāsit	The Expander
الخافض	Al-Khāfid	The Abaser
الرافع	Ar-Rāfi'	The Exalter
المعز	Al-Mu'izz	The Giver of Honour
المذل	Al-Mu'dhell	The Giver of Dishonour
السميع	As-Samī	The All Hearing
البصير	Al-Basīr	The All Seeing
الحكم	Al-Hakam	The Judge
العدل	Al-`Adl	The Utterly Just
اللطيف	Al-Latīf	The Gentle
الخبير	Al-Khabīr	The All Aware
الحليم	Al-Halīm	The Forbearing
العظيم	Al-'Azīm	The Magnificent
الغفور	Al-Ghafūr	The All Forgiving
الشكور	Ash-Shakūr	The Grateful
العلي	Al-'Aliyy	The Sublimely Exalted
الكبير	Al-Kabīr	The Great
الحفيظ	Al-Hafīz	The Preserver
المقيت	Al-Muqīt	The Nourisher
الحسيب	Al-Hasīb	The Bringer of Judgment
الجليل	Al-Jalīl	The Majestic
الكريم	Al-Karīm	The Bountiful
الرقيب	Ar-Raqīb	The Watchful
المجيب	Al-Mujīb	The Answerer

الواسع	Al-Wāsi'	The Vast
الحكيم	Al-Hakīm	The Wise
الودود	Al-Wadūd	The One who Loves
المجيد	Al-Majīd	The All Glorious
الباعث	Al-Bā'ith	The Raiser of The Dead
الشهيد	Ash-Shahīd	The Witness
الحق	Al-Haqq	The Truth
الوكيل	Al-Wakīl	The Trustee
القوى	Al-Qawwiyy	The Strong
المتين	Al-Matīn	The Firm
الولى	Al-Waliyy	The Protecting Friend
الحميد	Al-Hamid	The All Praiseworthy
المحصى	Al-Muhsi	The Accounter
المبدئ	Al-Mubdi'	The Producer
المعيد	Al-Mu'īd	The Restorer
المحيى	Al-Muhyi	The Giver of Life
المميت	Al-Mumīt	The Bringer of Death
الحي	Al-Hayy	The Ever Living
القيوم	Al-Qayyūm	The Self Subsisting Provider
الواجد	Al-Wājid	The Perceiver
الماجد	Al-Mājid	The Illustrious
الواحد	Al-Wāhid	The Unique
الاحد	Al-'Ahad	The One
الصمد	As-Samad	The Self Sufficient
القادر	Al-Qādir	The All Able
المقتدر	Al-Muqtadir	The Dominant

المقدم	Al-Muqaddim	The Expediter
المؤخر	Al-Mu'akhkhir	The Delayer
الأول	Al-'Awwal	The First (Alpha)
الأخر	Al-'Akhir	The Last (Omega)
الظاهر	Az-Zāhir	The All Victorious
الباطن	Al-Bātin	The Hidden
الوالي	Al-Wāli	The Patron
المتعالي	Al-Mutā'ali	The Self Exalted
البر	Al-Barr	The Most Kind and Righteous
التواب	At-Tawwāb	The Ever Returning
المنتقم	Al-Muntaqim	The Avenger
العفو	Al-Afuww	The Pardoner
الرؤوف	Ar-Ra'ūf	The Compassionate
مالك الملك	Mālik-ul-Mulk	The Owner of All Sovereignty
ذو الجلال والإكرام	Dhū-l-Jalāli-wa-l-'ikrām	The Lord of Majesty and Generosity
المقسط	Al-Muqsiṭ	The Equitable
الجامع	Al-Jāmi	The Gatherer
الغني	Al-Ghaniyy	The All Rich
المغني	Al-Mughni	The Enricher
المانع	Al-Māni'	The Defender
الضار	Ad-Dārr	The Afflictor
النافع	An-Nāfi	The Benefactor
النور	An-Nūr	The One Who Creates the Light
الهادي	Al-Hādi	The Guide
البديع	Al-Badī	The Incomparable
الباقى	Al-Bāqi	The Ever Enduring
الوارث	Al-Wārith	The Heir
الرشيد	Ar-Rashīd	The Guide
الصبور	As-Sabur	The Patient

Reading:

Allah is Al-Ahad, which means He is the one and only. Allah is the one and only creator, He has no partners. We learned that Allah was not born and that He will never die. And since He was not born that means that He has no mother or father. Since He will not die or grow old, He has no need of children to succeed Him or help Him during old age. Therefore, Allah has no wife, son, or daughter. Allah is One, alone, without partner; which in Arabic means Tawhid.

The Quran says:

قُلْ هُوَ ٱللَّهُ أَحَدٌ ۝١ ٱللَّهُ ٱلصَّمَدُ ۝٢

لَمْ يَلِدْ وَلَمْ يُولَدْ ۝٣ وَلَمْ يَكُن لَّهُۥ كُفُوًا أَحَدٌۢ ۝٤

Say: He is Allah, the One! Allah, the Eternal Refuge. He neither begets nor is born, And there is none comparable unto Him [Al-Ikhlas:1-4].

Allah created human beings. Some have special talents and gifts from Allah, but no human is perfect. All humans are born, and they all will die. They all need to eat, drink, and sleep for survival. Only Allah is perfect, and needs nothing to exist. Allah is not a human being and has no need for any of these things. We should never say that any human being is Allah, or a son of Allah. No human can be a partner of Allah either. Allah is the creator of all, and He is not created by anyone.

We should not believe that any human being is a god. It is wrong to worship any of the following:

- Creatures such as angels or animals
- Created objects such as trees, stones, mountains, or the sun
- Man-made objects such as idols, statues, or pictures
- Imaginary gods and spirits

In every prayer we use the words of Surah Al-Fatihah:

إِيَّاكَ نَعْبُدُ وَإِيَّاكَ نَسْتَعِينُ ۝٥

It is You we worship and You we ask for help [Al-Fatihah:5].

All of us come from Allah and one day we will return to Him. Life is our journey back to our Creator. We begin this journey as babies, helpless and dependent on our parents to take care of us and love us. They teach us the difference between right and wrong and the ways of the world. As we grow older our experiences of the world make us wiser and as adults we can take care of ourselves.

As adults we are strong and independent and often feel like nothing can hurt us. Eventually our bodies become weak and our health often makes us dependent on others once again, almost helpless, like we were when we were babies. As we grow older, we get closer to the end of our time on earth. However, Allah alone decides life and death, and anyone's death can come at anytime.

Allah tells us in the Quran that we were put on this earth to worship Him alone and then to return to Him. That is why, when anyone dies, we say:

$$\text{الَّذِينَ إِذَآ أَصَابَتْهُم مُّصِيبَةٌ قَالُوٓاْ إِنَّا لِلَّهِ وَإِنَّآ إِلَيْهِ رَٰجِعُونَ ﴿١٥٦﴾}$$

Who, when disaster strikes them, say, "Indeed we belong to Allah, and indeed to Him we will return" [Baqarah:156]. So, we must always be ready to meet our Maker. We must do good deeds and win His favor to be included in those who will enter paradise. The Quran reminds us over and over about the falseness of any other Gods. It asks the worshipers of man-made objects, "Do you worship that you have carved yourself or have you taken unto you other besides Him to be your protectors, even such as have no power to protect themselves."

To the worshipers of heavenly bodies the Quran tells the story of Prophet Ibrahim: One night Ibrahim looked into the night sky and he saw a star and said, "This is my Lord." But when it set, or went away, he said, "I love not the setters." When he saw the moon rising, he said, "This is my Lord." But when it set he said, "If my Lord does not guide me I shall surely be of the people gone astray." When he saw the sun rising, he said, "This is greater." But when it set he said, "O my people, surely I quit that you associate. I have turned my face to Him who originated the heavens and the earth, a man of pure faith, I am not of the idolaters."

To be a Muslim, or to surrender oneself to God, it is necessary to believe in the oneness of God, in the sense that He is the only creator, preserver, nourisher, etc. Therefore, a Muslim must say the Shahada: "There is no God but Allah and Mohamad is the Messenger of Allah."

Exercises:

1 Why doesn't Allah need parents or children?

2 Can a human being be a god?

3 Name some of the things a Muslim should not worship and discuss why it is useless to worship them.

4 Where will we go when we die?

5 What is the phrase you say when someone dies?

Poem:

This Shahada is a sacred creed,
Live by it and you'll succeed,
And be a witness to the truth,
Though you be a child or youth.

Activity:

Write out the Shahada on a poster board. You can turn this into an art project by painting it. Hang it in your house.

How does a Muslim submit to Allah?

- A Muslim believes that "There is no God besides Allah, alone, with no partner.

- A Muslim agrees that Mohamed (p) is the Messenger of Allah.

- A Muslim, therefore, believes that the message brought by Prophet Mohamed (p) -the Quran- is truly Allah's final and perfect message to man, and that what is in it is for his education and guidance. He must, therefore, study the teachings and lessons of the Quran.

- A Muslim, therefore, worships Allah in the way Allah has prescribed in the Quran.

- A Muslim, therefore, tries to obey Allah's laws as prescribed in the Quran.

- A Muslim, therefore, is good to other people, behaves as Allah and the Prophet (p) taught, and avoids behavior they disapproved, as described in the Quran and the Hadith (the say ings of the Prophet (p)).

- If a Muslim makes a mistake and does wrong he should repent at once and resolve the problem. He should not repeat the wrong-doing.

Chapter 3:
Allah and Science

Lesson: To learn about the science behind Allah's creation.

وَمِنْ ءَايَٰتِهِۦ خَلْقُ ٱلسَّمَٰوَٰتِ وَٱلْأَرْضِ وَمَا بَثَّ فِيهِمَا مِن دَآبَّةٍ وَهُوَ عَلَىٰ جَمْعِهِمْ إِذَا يَشَآءُ قَدِيرٌ ۩

"And among His Signs is the creation of the heavens and the earth, and the living creatures that He scattered through them, and He has Power to gather them together when He wills" [Ash-Shura:29].

Animals: Can you guess how many animals are part of the animal kingdom? There are thousands! They live in trees, under logs, in caves, in the ocean, on land, underground, and all over the globe. God created them all. All animals that live have a purpose in the animal kingdom. That means they all have something important to do while here on earth.

Purpose of animals: Have you ever heard of the aphid? It is an insect, which feeds on the plants. Ladybugs have a special job to help control the aphid population. Did you know that owls do more than just hoot? They help control the mice and rodent population by eating mice and other small animals. There is even an animal that can keep your garden free of snails and other petty creatures. It is called a hedgehog. It is important that these animals have the opportunity to do their job on this earth. Each of them plays a part in giving balance to the plant and animal kingdom.

We humans must do our best to preserve the habitats of animals because without a place to live animals may become endangered or extinct.

Every living animal gets its energy from the food it eats. The passing of energy from one living thing to another is called the food chain. It begins with the sun. When the sun shines on earth, plants gather the sun's energy and use it to produce food for themselves. Small animals eat the plants and get the energy, then bigger animals eat the smaller animals and the energy is passed on. It continues all the way up the food chain.

Example of a food chain: In a pond algae gathers sunlight to make food, then a small fish eats the algae, then a bird eats the small fish, then a bigger mammal might catch the bird and eat it. All living things have ways to make more of their own kind. This is called reproduction. Also a living creature must live where it is easy and where it can grow and develop. The place it lives in is called its environment. The environment will determine the kind of behavior of the animal.

Animals have instinct. Instinct is the ability to do something without having been taught to do it. Just like breathing or crying. Many animals have the ability to learn too. They can learn from trainers who repeat patterns and give them rewards.

41

Chapter 3:

Activities

Poems

&

Exercises

Exercises:

1 Where are different places animals can live?

2 Who created animals?

3 Where does energy begin?

4 What is it called when energy is passed from one living thing to another?

5 Which animal gets its energy from eating algae?

6 What is an animal's instinct?

Activity:

Draw a picture of an animal that you know and its habitat (environment).

Animal Covering Chart:

Many animals have coverings.

Fur
Skunks, Beavers

Scales
Reptiles, Sharks, Snakes

Feathers
Birds, Turkeys

Hair
Horses, Tarantula

Quills
Porcupine

Shells
Armadillo, Snails

Activity:

Animals can change color:

Some animals change colors as the seasons change and as the colors of their surroundings change. For example, the Arctic Fox and Hare have a thick white coat in the winter but in the spring they shed and their fur turns brown by the summer. Animals change color for many reasons like to protect their babies and to hide from animals when they hunt.

Fill in the missing letters:

Some animals change _ _ _ _ _.

They change color as the _ _ _ _ _ _ _ change.

They also change color as their _ _ _ _ _ _ _ _ _ _ _ _ _ _ change.

The white fur of the Arctic _ _ _ and _ _ _ _ turn _ _ _ _ _ in the summer.

Reading:
Interesting facts about birds:

Allah created birds with traits that suit their environment.

The Quran says: Do they not look at the birds, held poised in the midst of (the air and) the sky? Nothing holds them up but the Power of God. Truly in this are Signs for those who believe [An-Nahl:79].

When God created hawks, He gave them eyes perfectly suited to hunting. Certain hawks have eyes, which are eight times sharper than ours.

They can spot a mouse in a field one-half mile away. Because both eyes are placed in the front of a hawk's head, they work together to judge distances. A bird swooping down from the sky must know exactly how close the ground is. A hawk hardly ever crash-lands. Its eyes are placed just right to prevent that.

A **sparrow** never dives for food. It sits and eats seeds. So it has been given eyes set farther apart. It can't judge distances well. But it can spot enemies coming from the front or either side.

A **cardinal's** beak isn't sensitive. The seeds that it eats don't move and are in plain view. But they can be tough at times. So Allah gave the cardinal a short stout beak for cracking seeds.

A **woodcock's** bill is perfectly suited for grubbing in mud. It's long so the bird's face doesn't get dirty. The tip is sensitive enough to feel slight movements in the mud. A woodcock finds its meals by touch.

A **duck** needs a bigger beak to grab plants it finds when it dives into the water. Its broad, flat bill is perfect for this. It even has a little strainer along the sides. A duck can strain out water and keep in plants. As it swims, a duck needs all the power it can get. So it has webbed feet, built in flippers, created specially to help a duck swim.

A **crossbill** is the only kind of bird that can pick seeds from cones. Its bill was created perfectly for that.

Activity:

Next time you are outside, bring a pine cone home and try to pull the seeds out with a pair of tweezers.

Reading:
Interesting facts about ants:

- Ants are considered a marvel of creation. Ants are almost all females. Male ants are only produced once in a great while and quickly die. All the worker ants as well as the queen ants are female.

- Ants communicate with each other and have their own language.

- The Arabic word for ant is Al Naml. In the Quran, Allah says that Prophet Suleiman heard an ant speaking to other ants telling them to run and hide to avoid being stepped on.

- When telling this story, Allah said "Qalat," which is the feminine verb of "said." This was before anyone on earth studied ants and knew that most of them were female.

Interesting facts about bats:

- Bats eat fruit and bugs. In one night they can catch thousands of insects.

- Bats have a built-in air conditioner, They have a fur coat but when they fly with their wings their blood in cooled as it flows through those wings.

- They have a sonar that helps them find food in the darkest night.

- They squeal high-pitched squeaks several times a second. The echoes bounce off bugs right back to you. Their big ears help them tell the squeaks from the echoes so they can zero in on their food.

Interesting facts about snakes:

- Snakes have jaws that hear. The bone that translates sound waves into sound are connected to the jaw. They pick up vibrations from the ground.

- Their jaw unhinges so they can swallow their food whole, like a rat or bird.

- Snakes have tongues that smell. Inside their mouth are two holes that match the tongue tips. These holes have lots of smelling cells. The tongue picks up molecules of odor from the air then puts them in to the two holes. The smelling cells tell the snake what's nearby.

- Snakes don't have arms, legs, or ear holes.

Activity:

To feel how a snake catches food, put an apple on the floor, the get down on your belly about 5 feet away from the apple.

Then put your arms against your body and slither to the apple. Try biting in the apple without using your hands.

Reading: Space:

The sky over us and the space around us are all part of Allah's creation.

Whether you live in the United States or Morocco, you can go outside and look up at the sky and see the sun, the moon, stars, and if you look through a telescope (a machine that lets you look at things millions of miles away) different planets, comets, and meteors. Scientists have taught us a lot about these things.

And most of this information is written in the Quran.

Allah created the universe. Everything was compacted together and then split apart. Gases spread throughout the universe and stars, planets, and other things were formed.

This is what is called the big bang. The Quran refers to the start of the big bang in two short Ayahs presenting an accurate summary to the conditions that led to creating the universe:

Do not the unbelievers see that the heavens and the earth were joined together (as one unit of creation) before We clove them asunder? [Al-'Anbya':30].

Then He turned to the sky and it had been (as) smoke [Fussilat:11].

The Sun:

Energy comes from the sun. The sun keeps our earth warm. It is very very far from the Earth. The heat and light from the sun travels a long distance to reach us. Sunshine is very important to everything on Earth. The Quran says:

وَٱلشَّمْسِ وَضُحَىٰهَا ﴿١﴾

وَٱلْقَمَرِ إِذَا تَلَىٰهَا ﴿٢﴾

وَٱلنَّهَارِ إِذَا جَلَّىٰهَا ﴿٣﴾

وَٱلَّيْلِ إِذَا يَغْشَىٰهَا ﴿٤﴾

By the sun and its brightness And [by] the moon when it follows it. And [by] the day when it displays it. And [by] the night when it covers it [Ash-Shams:1-4]

It also says:

هُوَ ٱلَّذِى جَعَلَ لَكُمُ ٱلَّيْلَ لِتَسْكُنُوا۟ فِيهِ وَٱلنَّهَارَ مُبْصِرًا إِنَّ فِى ذَٰلِكَ لَءَايَٰتٍ لِّقَوْمٍ يَسْمَعُونَ ﴿٦٧﴾

It is He who made for you the night to rest therein and the day, giving sight. Indeed in that are signs for a people who listen [Yunus:67].

تُولِجُ ٱلَّيْلَ فِى ٱلنَّهَارِ وَتُولِجُ ٱلنَّهَارَ فِى ٱلَّيْلِ وَتُخْرِجُ ٱلْحَىَّ مِنَ ٱلْمَيِّتِ وَتُخْرِجُ ٱلْمَيِّتَ مِنَ ٱلْحَىِّ وَتَرْزُقُ مَن تَشَآءُ بِغَيْرِ حِسَابٍ ﴿٢٧﴾

And: You cause the night to enter the day, and You cause the day to enter the night; and You bring the living out of the dead, and You bring the dead out of the living. And You give provision to whom You will without account [Al-Imran:27].

At night the sun shines on the other side of the Earth. Then our half is dark and begins to cool. Therefore, the temperature changes from day to night.

The United States is between the equator and the north pole. The temperature at the north and south poles is severely cold all year long. The sun shines on the entire earth, but some parts get more heat than others.

Solar System:

The solar system is made of the sun, moon, comets, and nine planets. Each planet travels in its own space around the sun called the planet's orbit. Some planets are large, some are small, some are very close to the sun and some are very far.

Mercury

Mercury is the smallest planet. It is very hot.

Venus

Venus is known as the evening or morning star, it gives the brightest light in the solar system after the sun and moon.

Earth

Earth is our home. The planet is mostly water and has plants and animals. It is about 93,000,000 miles from the sun. It has oxygen and a mixture of gases such as nitrogen and helium.

Mars

Mars is a small planet close to earth. It is known as the twin to earth because they both have oxygen, water, polar caps and the length of the day and night are about the same.

Jupiter

Jupiter is the largest planet. It has a poisonous atmosphere, no oxygen or water. It is freezing cold day and night.

Saturn

Saturn is called the ringed planet. It is a very cold planet.

Uranus

Uranus is extremely cold. It is made of gas and looks bluish-green because of the chemicals it is made from. It is surrounded by 9 rings made from rocks and ice.

Neptune

Neptune is a very cold planet as well. Like Uranus, it is made of gas and looks bluish-green because of the chemicals is it made from.

Pluto (dwarf planet)

Pluto is much smaller than any of the official planets and is now classified as a "dwarf planet."

Internet Activity:

Draw a diagram of the solar system. To make it easier, look one up using Google.

Exercise:

1   List all planets in order from the sun.

2   What is the orbit of a planet?

3   How many miles away are we from the sun?

4   Which planet is called the "twin" of earth?

5   Which planet is called the "ringed planet"?

The Moon:

The moon is a satellite of the earth. Which means it revolves around the earth very closely. The moon goes around the Earth once every month. As the moon moves around the earth, the part facing us changes.

There are holes in the moon called craters. Some say these holes were made from meteors. A meteor is a rock or metal that travels through space. A comet is made from gases, ice and specks of dust that travel through space. Comets are much larger than meteors; infact a meteor is simply a speck of dust from a comet. Most meteors are small and burn away before reaching earth. But some are big enough to survive and fall on our land. A landed meteor is called a meteorite. They can make a hole in the round called a crater.

There is a crater in Arizona about half a mile wide and 575 feet deep. It was made over 22,000 years ago.

Internet Activity:

Using Google, look up information with a parent about this crater in Arizona and write one paragraph about it.

Stars:

A star is a huge mass of hot gas. Allah says in the Quran:

وَهُوَ ٱلَّذِى جَعَلَ لَكُمُ ٱلنُّجُومَ لِتَهْتَدُوا۟ بِهَا فِى ظُلُمَٰتِ ٱلْبَرِّ وَٱلْبَحْرِ قَدْ فَصَّلْنَا ٱلْءَايَٰتِ لِقَوْمٍ يَعْلَمُونَ ﴿٩٧﴾

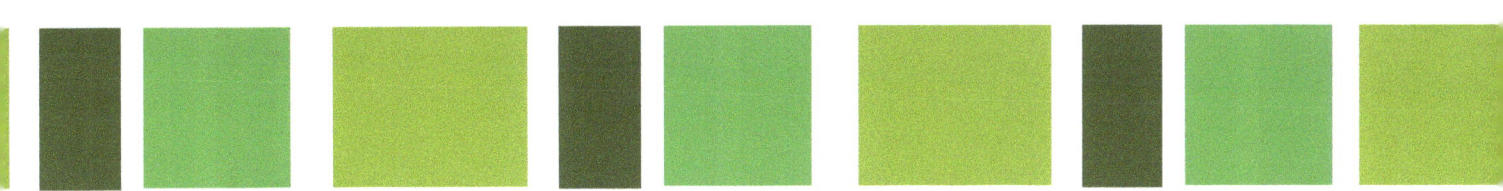

And it is He who placed for you the stars that you may be guided by them through the darkness of the land and sea. We have detailed the signs for a people who know [Al-'An`am:97].

The stars are placed in a way that give you direction. For example the star seen in the North in called Polaris. It is in the same place everyday.

It is also called the Night Star. It determines the four directions: North, South, East, and West.

When you look up at the sky on a clear night, you can see 22,000 stars with just your own eyes.

With a telescope you can see millions of stars in just one small part of the sky. So you can imagine how many stars there are?

Stars come in many colors. The temperature of the star gives it its color. A blue star is the hottest, over 19,000 degrees Fahrenheit.

The sun is a star! It is a medium-hot star. Its color is yellow. Its temperature is 10,000 degrees Fahrenheit.

Even though you may think that stars are small, they are actually very big!

They are bigger than the earth and bigger than Jupiter, which is the largest planet. They are among the largest of Allah's creation.

Imagine this: if our sun was hollow on the inside, more than a million earths could fit inside. Some stars are so big that more than a million of our sun could fit in to them!

Stars are very far away as you can imagine. The closest star to earth that is visible at night is 25 trillion miles away.

There are groups of stars called constellations. These create shapes and are given names accordingly. The Quran says:

تَبَارَكَ ٱلَّذِى جَعَلَ فِى ٱلسَّمَآءِ بُرُوجًا وَجَعَلَ فِيهَا سِرَٰجًا وَقَمَرًا مُّنِيرًا ﴿٦١﴾

Blessed is the One who places the constellation in the heaven and placed therein a lamp and a moon giving light." [Al-Furqan-61].

Does this give you an idea of just how large the universe is?

Water:

Water is the basis of all life. Allah created all life from water. The earth is 2/3 water, most of it is in the oceans. There are 3 forms of water: solid, liquid, gas. When water changes its form its weight does not change. So when water changes to ice it weighs the same, and when it changes to steam it weighs the same.

Water is important because it helps everything grow and keeps things clean.

Our fresh water comes from lakes, rivers, and wells. And the oceans have salt water. The Quran says:

وَهُوَ ٱلَّذِى مَرَجَ ٱلْبَحْرَيْنِ هَٰذَا عَذْبٌ فُرَاتٌ وَهَٰذَا مِلْحٌ أُجَاجٌ وَجَعَلَ بَيْنَهُمَا بَرْزَخًا وَحِجْرًا مَّحْجُورًا ﴿٥٣﴾

And it is He who has released [simultaneously] the two seas, one fresh and sweet and one salty and bitter, and He placed between them a barrier and prohibiting partition [Al-Furqan:53].

All plants and animals need water to stay alive. In fact Allah created us from water. The Quran says:

وَهُوَ ٱلَّذِى خَلَقَ مِنَ ٱلْمَاءِ بَشَرًا فَجَعَلَهُۥ نَسَبًا وَصِهْرًا وَكَانَ رَبُّكَ قَدِيرًا ﴿٥٤﴾

And it is He who has created from water a human being and made him [a relative by] lineage [Al-Furqan:54]. And:

أَوَلَمْ يَرَ ٱلَّذِينَ كَفَرُوٓا۟ أَنَّ ٱلسَّمَٰوَٰتِ وَٱلْأَرْضَ كَانَتَا رَتْقًا فَفَتَقْنَٰهُمَا وَجَعَلْنَا مِنَ ٱلْمَاءِ كُلَّ شَىْءٍ حَىٍّ أَفَلَا يُؤْمِنُونَ ﴿٣٠﴾

Have those who disbelieved not considered that the heavens and the earth were a joined entity, and We separated them and made from water every living thing? Then will they not believe? [Al-'Anbya':30]. Water is mentioned in the Quran 32 times!

Exercises:

1 Why is water so important?

2 Which bodies of water are fresh and which are salty?

3 How many times is water mentioned in the Quran?

Plants:

Plants are important. We use plants everyday.

We eat the fruits and veggies they produce, we build houses from the wood of trees, we use the paper from the wood of trees, we use cotton from the cotton seed and make clothes, we look at the beautiful flowers, etc.

There are four things a seed needs to grow into a plant: air, water, warmth (sun), and minerals.

Plants go through a growth process called photosynthesis where energy is converted into food through the leaves. When the sunlight hits the plant, it creates energy from the water and air.

The Quran says:

﴿ وَهُوَ ٱلَّذِىٓ أَنشَأَ جَنَّـٰتٍ مَّعْرُوشَـٰتٍ وَغَيْرَ مَعْرُوشَـٰتٍ وَٱلنَّخْلَ وَٱلزَّرْعَ مُخْتَلِفًا أُكُلُهُۥ وَٱلزَّيْتُونَ وَٱلرُّمَّانَ مُتَشَـٰبِهًا وَغَيْرَ مُتَشَـٰبِهٍۚ كُلُواْ مِن ثَمَرِهِۦٓ إِذَآ أَثْمَرَ وَءَاتُواْ حَقَّهُۥ يَوْمَ حَصَادِهِۦۖ وَلَا تُسْرِفُوٓاْ إِنَّهُۥ لَا يُحِبُّ ٱلْمُسْرِفِينَ ﴿١٤١﴾

And He it is who causes gardens to grow, [both] trellised and untrellised, and palm trees and crops of different [kinds of] food and olives and pomegranates, similar and dissimilar. Eat of (each of) its fruit when it yields and give its due (zakah) on the day of its harvest. And be not excessive. Indeed, He does not like those who commit excess [Al-An'am:141].

Activity:

Go to the store with your parent and buy a seed to plant at home.

Conclusion:

When you study geography and science, you can learn a lot about how these things work.

The more you know about how they work, the more you will marvel at Allah's arrangement, power, and wisdom. Despite all the knowledge that science, geography, and other disciplines provide mankind, there is a wealth of knowledge that remains untapped, only to be known by Allah.

That is what scientists refer to as the "mysteries of life." Perhaps Allah may choose to unravel these mysteries some day. Until then, we must continue our search for His signs and try to gain wisdom in what He has provided us.

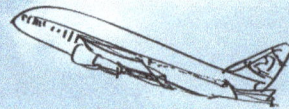

Many books have been written to help children learn about and love Allah. We hope that this compilation of our own work and many other great resources benefits you and your family.

Answers to Exercises:

Chapter 1:

Set 1:
1. Allah
2. Al-Baqi-The Everlasting, Al-Rabb-The Sustainer
3. No
4. No
5. Al-Hayy-The Ever Living One, Al-Khaliq-The Creator
6. Al-Awwal-The First, Al-Akhir-The Last
7. His command is only when He intends a thing that He says to it, "Be," and it is [36:82]; Surah Yasin, Ayah 82

Set 2:
1. Allah
2. Al-Bari
3. Because He created everything.
4. Al-Musawwir
5. Yes
6. No

Chapter 2:

Set 1:
1. Allah was not born, that means that He has no mother or father. Since He will not die or grow old, He has no need of children to succeed Him or help Him during old age.
2. No
3. Man made objects, creatures; because Allah created them all.
4. We return to our Creator.
5. "Indeed we belong to Allah, and indeed to Him we will return."

Chapter 3:

Set 1:
1. Caves, trees, ocean
2. Allah
3. Sun
4. Food chain
5. Small fish
6. The ability to do something without having been taught to do it.

Set 2:
1. Mercury, Venus, Earth, Mars, Jupiter, Saturn, Uranus, Neptune, Pluto.
2. Each planet's own space around the sun.
3. 93,000,000
4. Mars
5. Saturn

Set 3:
1. It is the basis of all life.
2. Fresh: lakes, rivers, and wells; Salty: oceans
3. 32

www.ingramcontent.com/pod-product-compliance
Lightning Source LLC
Chambersburg PA
CBHW081141090426
42736CB00018B/3440